Where There's Hope = There's Love

POEMS OF HOPE & LOVE FOR TODAY & TOMORROW

by

Doris Washington

Book Cover & Interior Photographs by Joni Meyers
Author Photograph is supplied by the Author

Library of Congress Control Number: 2018906872
ISBN: Hardcover   978-1-9845-3408-8
                 Softcover   978-1-9845-3409-5
                 eBook   978-1-9845-3410-1

Book Cover & Interior Photographs by Joni Meyers
Author Photograph is supplied by the Author

Print information available on the last page.

Rev. date: 06/30/2018

To order additional copies of this book, contact:
Xlibris
1-888-795-4274
www.Xlibris.com
Orders@Xlibris.com
780612

Contents

GATHERING STONES

HIS EVERLASTING LOVE

AS I PLANT THE SEEDS OF MY GARDEN

A RAINBOW OF HOPE

OVER THE HORIZON

CLOSING POEM

Dedication

I dedicate this book to my loving and devoted husband John, And to my precious son John.

Acknowledgements

There are some wonderful people that I would like to thank so much for making this work all possible. For your support and love is a godsend. To my husband and son John, thank you for blessing my life, each and every day. I thank God for you. To my friends Audrey & Raymond Edwards, I thank you for your wonderful support always. And I thank my mother Emma Buchanan, for her unconditional love she always gives. And to all my many wonderful friends and family, thank you so much for all your support.

Foreword

Where There's Hope – There's Love is a collection of poems, that inspire us with hope for today and tomorrow. It is a collection of poems of inner peace for the soul, positive thinking, holding on to hope and trusting in faith, that God will see us through the challenges of life's experiences, that no matter the challenges we face in the present day, will pass, for even brighter tomorrows.   Also, in this collection, as a mother of an adult son with autism, I wanted to share a positive side in looking at autism, which I so express in the poems, *Do You See You Him? Do You Hear Him? Do You Know Him? / Tears* and *John.*

In my poems *God's Enduring Love* and *Over the Horizon,* I share as we trust in faith, that God will see us through any storm and to believe in faith that, today may not be your tomorrow.   In my poem *Gathering Stones,* I share through our healing we gather stones to begin again. And through my poem *Let Love Take You,* I share we can begin again by discovering the love in our hearts through healing and forgiveness. In my two poems *Today Not Be Your Tomorrow,* and *Where's There's Hope- There's Love,* I share that with hope to hold on to, that no matter what each day brings, we can find peace within.

And in my closing poem *Beyond the Sunset,* I share that as we discover love, we will have a most beautiful world, as we come to Love. May this book, Where There's Hope- There's Love, inspire us to hold on to hope and to discover the beauty of Love.

Poems About Autism

Do You See Him? Do You Hear Him? Do You Know Him?

Do You See Him?
He is My Child-and he is dear to me.
He has Autism, an Invisible Disability.

Do You Hear Him?
You may not understand why he does not quickly
Respond to you.
For he is not bad, he is just different from what you are used to.

Do you Know Him?
You may find he will need more time to do a certain task.
And if there are too many demands, please understand they may be
Difficult for him to grasp.

For there are other places I could have chose for him to live.
I made the choice for him to stay with
me, for I see what he can give.

He may not understand danger. I worry if he will be safe.
And as I struggle with the many difficulties,
and challenges, *I Keep The Faith.*

I only ask for him – One Request!

Please Learn About Him.

So he can have a chance to give his best.

Do You See Him? Do You Hear Him? Do You Know Him?

Tears

Many times for you I cry tears.
And the struggle goes on,
I Cry! I Pray!
To believe someday,
You'll have a place too!
Many times for you I cry tears,
When the world doesn't understand
All about you-I Cry! I Pray!
Hoping you will not waste away
With your beautiful soul,
That some don't always see.
Many times for you I cry tears.
When it's not easy to explain,
Why today you're not doing well,
And you can't express with words
How you feel.
Many times for you I cry tears.
For a great understanding of your
Uniqueness, and worth.
As I accept you exactly as you are -
I Cry! I Pray! Others will too!

Many times for you I cry tears.
And the struggle goes on.
I Cry! I Pray!

To believe someday,
You'll have a place too!
Many times for you I Cry-
Tears.

John

You are a precious child,
For you have been sent from God above.
You are the joy of my life.
For you have taught me how to *Love.*

You brighten up the day
With your everlasting smile.
I am so proud to have you as my son.
For you help make my life worthwhile.

As I hear your sweet melody of songs you sing.
It could be a spiritual or popular tune or too.
How beautiful and special you are.
For this is all-What Makes You!

You make my life worth living.
And I keep going each and everyday.
How important you are to me – So true.
As I look forward to everyday.
And I hear you say: "God is with us."
And I respond: "All the time."
I could not imagine my life without you.
My Precious Son –
John

Sunrise

Hold on to Hope for brighter tomorrows –
Each time the sun rises.

As The Morning Comes

At this moment I start anew-
Releasing all worries-
I find strength for the day.
For with You –
I can overcome any obstacle.

And as I face each day-
I Pray-
Leaving all with You!
I see the joy more than before.
And for each day You give me-
I thank You more each time –
The Morning Comes.

Each Day I Awake

The world is most beautiful
When the sun shines on a-
Snow-capped winter's morning.

The world is most beautiful
When spring is in full bloom-
Trees of Cherry Blossoms-
And gardens of flowers all around.

The world is most beautiful
When summer nights showcase the stars above-
No matter where you are.

The world is most beautiful
When autumn leaves keep falling
On those cool days, just before winter.

And the world is most beautiful-
Each day I awake-
I still see *Love* no matter
Where I may be-
I see *Love* –
With the hope for an even brighter tomorrow-
Each Day I Awake.

A New Day

I awake from a long sleep,
Yes, a long sleep from loneliness,
Self pity,
And regret.
I no longer choose to taste the bitter tongue
Of the trials of life.

I no longer allow worry, self-doubt,
And negative energy to be the focus of existence.
I no longer starve for others approval,
Opinions and love.

Forgiveness is what I practice.
Patience has become my daily routine.
Love keeps me alive.
And I seek Him always.
As I Start-
A New Day

The Morning Sun

Revelations came to me
At the break of dawn.
Realizing many things.
Looking over my life,
How it has been,
Where I am now,
And where I am going.
Letting go of issues from others,
Issues I have, I'm facing
What I can't change.
And I'm moving forward to a new change.
My healing begins.
And I can see clear,
As I see-
The Morning Sun

A New Day Begins

Life is always changing-
And a new day begins.
Life has its challenges,
Its joys.
The good news is while
You're here there's always
The opportunity to live
Each day as if it's your last.
Take each experience
And always see the blessing
Behind every one.
Sometimes things don't always
Work out as we hope.
But never give up on *Hope.*
Sometimes the rain comes
To make room for the sun to shine
Even brighter.
For life is always changing-
And-
A New Day Begins!

As Tomorrow Comes

Hope may seem difficult to hold on to.
And whatever challenges you may
Experience at the present day,
Know it's a temporary thing.
For today may not be your tomorrow.

Hold on to *Hope* when it seems
Difficult to do so.
Just Hold On.
And believe the sun will rise again.
Yes!
The sun will rise-
As Tomorrow Comes.

Through And Beyond The Storm

See the sun as the storm comes.

He brings hope through it all.

Hold on to it always.

Trust in Him.

He's always there.

Sometimes Life can bring many challenges.

Sometimes all at once.

And whatever comes to be,

Know it will pass.

Hold on and Pray.

For as the storm comes,

Know He'll always be there-

Through and Beyond.

Morning

Yesterday has come and gone.
Tomorrow brings promise,
And always hope.
And for now,
I'm doing alright.
Yes! I'm doing just fine.
And each breath I take-
It's Good!
Yes! –
It's All Good!
Hello-
Morning!

The Joy In The Morning

Life has its storms.
And there's always the joy in the morning
That can carry you through the night,
And the next day after that.
When problems arise,
And there seems no relief.
Hold on to the joy.
Let the sun shine through.
Believe it all takes care of itself,
No matter the storm.
And you'll find peace.
For Life has its Storms.
And there's always –
The Joy In The Morning!

Avenues

Alone, I walk in the morning sun,
I find there're many roads to venture to.
Not sure where I'm going,
For there're many directions
To follow through.

With so much before me,
I find things can change
From one minute to the next.
And I'm learning life
Is all about passing the test.

I ask the Lord to be my teacher.
I ask the Lord to be my guide.
And no matter what my life may be-
I feel His Love inside.

Alone, I walk in the morning sun,
I find there're many roads to venture to.
Not sure where I'm going,
For there're many directions
To follow through.
There Are Many-
Avenues.

Sunrise

As the sun rises each morning so new.
I Thank God for another day.
For on this day I choose to live each moment
Even better than the day before.
And right now-I have a chance to do all that
I hope for-dream for.

Life is so precious.
Each moment counts.
And what's more beautiful for each day I awake-
I can change things always for the better.
Whether it's to make things right with someone-
Or whether it's to fulfill my true passion in life-
Each time the sun rises-
Each Morning So New.

God's Enduring Love

The sun will always shine through the rain.
For it's the reassurance of God's Enduring Love.

Today May Not Be Your Tomorrow

With each new day,
And for what it may bring –
Always have *Hope*.
What may be now-
Can change tomorrow.
Pray!

Even if it seems things are not
Getting better-
Trust in Him most of all.
For He can bring a miracle
In any given moment.
There's always a blessing
Through the storm.

Never stop believing.
For where there's sadness and despair-
There's joy and always triumph.
You'll never know what each day will bring.
Always hold on to-*Hope*.
For *Today* may not be your-*tomorrow*.

A Time, A Season, And Always Love

I pray more than ever now,
At a time where perceptions,
And what's on the surface
Has more weight, I pray for Love.

I pray for a revaluation of thoughts
To see love and believe in it so.

For each season,
Each winter as the snow falls,
Each spring as the flowers blossom,
And the trees grow,
Each summer as more sunny
And warm days appear,
Each fall as the leaves fall,
And the cool winds fill the air,
I pray for each time,
Each season for love to stay.

I pray for a time where the act of trust,
And faith in humankind becomes more present,
Especially now.
I pray for Love to stay always,
Yes! Always!

I Pray for-
A Time, A Season, And Always Love.

God's Promise

There're days the sun will shine so beautiful.
There're days the storms will come –
That may seem to last forever.
And for what each day brings-
His Promise is that He'll be there always.

As you trust in God's Enduring Love-
As you believe He can do all things possible-
You will see the blessings He brings-
Through the sunshine and through the rain.

God's Promise is not always in your time-
But always in His Time.
And as you believe in Him-
You'll always have the joy in the morning-
And the faith that His Mercy-His Love will never fail you.

There're days the sun will shine so beautiful.
There're days the storms will come-
That may seem to last forever.
And what each day brings-
Stay in faith He'll be there.
Always-
God's Promise.

May Peace Be With You

As the morning breaks on this most beautiful day-
I rest my heart with no heavy sorrow.
Only such wonderful thoughts I hold dear of you.
And with every joyous moment while you were here-
I hold on to the understanding it was your time to go.

Each day I find peace.
I cherish the times no matter how brief.
I am blessed with the joy you brought –
And much more.

Sometimes we may not understand why
Those we love cannot stay?
But as we cherish what they have given
To us-whether it be inspiration or – Joy! –
We can find peace.

And as each day passes –
As we remember the beauty of what
They brought to our lives-
As we remember them-
May Peace Be with You.

Jesus My Friend Forever More

Let me tell you about my friend Jesus.
His Love is here today and *Always*.
He gives me a second chance,
A third chance,
A fourth chance to get it right.
He cares for me.

Let me tell you about my friend Jesus.
He has given me salvation like no other.
I can count on Him each and every time.
For His Mercy-
His Kindness-
His Compassion is so true.
He cares for me.

Let me tell you about my friend Jesus.
Who will never let you down.
When you need a friend to talk to
He listens,
He comforts you and holds your hand.
He cares for me.

Let me tell you about my friend Jesus.
For if you lose your way,
Do not worry-

Do not be afraid-
Just trust in Him.
And know that His Light is the reassurance-
He's a friend forever more.
Oh!-How He Cares for Me!

The Most Beautiful Gift

Life itself is a blessing.
And there'll be disappointments
Along the way.

And for every –
Challenge you so endure-
Find the joy and peace within.

Hold on to every blessing-
And begin to love you.
Follow your passion-
No matter where it takes you.

For each day you have begins
With you and how you live life.
And the most beautiful gift
Is the *Love* you give each
And every time you breathe – *Life!*

Only Love

Love is the answer to all things.
For as one heart that has love,
Inspires many hearts to know love.
Love is far better to have than all
The Wealth,
The Fame,
And Statue in Life.
Only Love can conquer all.
Love can change the world
Beyond imagination.
Love Forgives,
Listens,
And hears with the heart.
There's nothing that can surpass Love.
Love! –
It's the answer to all things.

His Amazing Love

My Lord!-
You're my strength-my song.
You're the joy in the morning –
My healer of all my hurts-my pains-
You're my salvation.

For no matter what I go through.
For no matter what each day may bring-
You keep blessing me through it all.

My Lord!
You not only heal-
You're merciful-
And Yes!-
You're a fixer too!

For to trust in You I must.
With all my heart and soul-
I surrender it all.

My Lord!-
You're my strength-my song.
You're the joy in the morning-
My healer of all my hurts-my pains-
You're my salvation!
You keep blessing me through it all.
Oh! Your Amazing Love!

Thank You For This Day

Dear Lord-
I Thank You for this day.
This day as I begin a new-found journey.
Full of the promise and the faith I have found
With You.
I Thank You for each blessing You bestow upon me.
I sing with abounding joy of Your Love.
And as I awake each day,
I ask for Your Anointing –
Giving me the reassurance
That with-
Your Grace,
Your Mercy,
I can always begin again.
Dear Lord-
I Thank You for This Day.

God's Enduring Love

There'll be days full of clouds in the skies.
And there'll be days the sun shines so beautiful.
And for every moment we have-each day-
We can be thankful.

Life has its challenges-
Its *Joys*.
His Miracles are all around us
In the wake of each new day.

And as we endure and find strength for the day.
As we hold on to *faith-*
There's always *Hope* to see us through every storm.
There's Always-
God's Enduring Love.

Gathering Stones

As we pick up the broken pieces-gathering stones-
As we choose to live a better way-
Inner peace we'll embrace and come to know.

Let Love Take You

Always *Love* is there for you to discover.
And the more that you embrace *Love-*
The more you encourage others to discover it too.

There're times, when you spread the *Love-*
It's not always received by some.
But never stop giving up on *Love.*

What's so beautiful about *Love-*
Is that it never stops giving up on you-
To believe in it so.

The most important thing of all-
Is that you give the *Love.*
For it always starts with you.

As you start to see with *Love!* –
As you let go-
As you let *Love* take you-
You'll find that *Love-*
Will always find it's way back to you.

I Do Not Want To Hurt Anymore

I'm afraid.
Why?
I have been hurt.
And it seems as though things don't change.
What to do?

I feel at times I want to go away and hide.
Still I find that is not the answer.
Should I just avoid situations with those who can be cruel?
Still I find that is not the answer.
Should I just cry?
Oh, but that would make me sad.
And I have been there before.
Or should I just be mad?
And I have been there before too.
And I was unhappy.
And yet, I'm still afraid.
So, I Pray! And I Pray! And I Pray!

Maybe if I just learn to like myself.
I may come to see that I am someone.
Then maybe I can believe everything
Will be just fine.
For-
I Do Not Want To Hurt Anymore

Start Anew

When you start anew,
Just remember to keep you.
For each situation you journey is different.
And each one you meet is not the same.
Go into each experience leaving issues
Of the heart behind.
Let positive thoughts fill your mind.
Forgive, even if it's hard to do.
And just let Love take you,
When you-
Start Anew

Forgive

O Lord! Teach me how to forgive.
Show me the way to Love, a better way to live.

Lord! Sometimes I get confused,
And I'm not sure which way to go.

I lay my troubles on your shoulders,
Please help me to grow.

Dear Lord!
There are times when the world is unkind,
And I find myself in despair.

Please anoint me with your love.
Even when the world seems to not care.

Direct me in a positive way,
So, I can be example of goodness and grace.

I only want to know your way,
To guide me to the right place.
Dear Lord!
Please teach me how to-
Forgive

I Can Always Begin Again

My healing begins through forgiveness.
My hurt-my pain is washed away.
And as I find the *love*
Always inside of me-
I can begin again.
I can start anew.

He may close a door-
For another door to open.
And Life's twist and turns
May be too much to bear at times.
But as I lean on Him-
Trust in Him to know
He'll work it all out in time-
Oh! Such peace I find.

And with that I can see a new day
Always starts with me.
To understand what I cannot change -
I must surrender it all to Him.

My healing begins through forgiveness.
My hurt-my pain is washed away.
And as I fill my heart with His Love-
I Can Always Begin Again.

Whirlwind

In a whirlwind spinning
Out of control.
Finally stepping back
To see what direction
You're taking.
Is it good?
Is it right?
Understanding what is meant to be.
Revaluating all of it since it started,
And where it is now.
Then to realize for self,
That Acceptance is Peace.

Direction

Yesterday I cannot change,
But today I can.
And as I awake on this new morning-
I start again.

Mistakes are sometimes made
More often than not.
And I choose not to dwell on what is past.
But right now, I have a choice to live a better way.

Inner peace I so invite to have at all times.
I lean on Him always for guidance-for strength-
Each and every day.

Yesterday I cannot change,
But today I can.
And this choice to live a most positive life-
Is a *direction* I seek more and more.

Beyond The Clouds

As the day awakes-
I move forward to discover
There's always a *blessing*
To encourage me to look-
Beyond the clouds.

Peace within my soul-
I seek more than ever now-
In a vast and ever changing world-
Where negativity abounds.

I feel my heart with love.
And with a positive way of living-
I can see the blessings He gives to me
In every moment of the day.
And I see that life is more beautiful-
More fulfilled this way.
As I look –
Beyond The Clouds.

Letting Go

Cleansing in one's soul.

Peace,

And serenity flows.

Hurt,

And pain released.

Your heart at peace.

Love steps in,

As you surrender it to Him.

Letting Go!

The Beauty Of Love

As you love, you live fulfilled.
And as you give love, you encourage
Others to give too.
But remember, there're times when love
May not be accepted or received by some.
And sometimes you may feel if it's worth the try.
But just stop and think
As you turn a negative situation
To a positive one,
You'll find much peace, much joy
You can ever imagine when you always
Answer to your heart.
Can you ever imagine anything greater?
For that's-
The Beauty of Love.

Peace

Sometimes forgiving can be difficult,
Especially when feeling hurt and disappointed.
Sometimes even when the world is unkind,
Being right doesn't hold too much.
Letting go can be such a wonderful feeling,
And the world will seem much nicer.
It's a matter of perspective.
It's a matter how to deal with it
In your mind-in your heart-in your soul.
To let go with no hesitation for the simple
Reason to be at-
Peace.

The Beauty Of Life

Sometimes there are moments
Through life's journey things just happen
With no explanation.
And I have found that when I truly let go –
To come to peace –
Life is so beautiful.

For when things are not going so well-
And when it seems as if all is falling apart-
I find only when I let go of those things
I cannot change-I come to peace.

At this moment, I come to peace.
For no matter, what I go through.
No matter the joys and the trials-
I come to peace.
And more than ever I find-
Life is So Beautiful.

Gathering Stones

Recovering from it all,
I pick up the broken pieces
Along the way.
Drifting away far too long,
I now re-group, to get some balance.
And I'm ready to begin again.

There's so much out here
To discover.
And yet I feel uncertain where
I'm going.
Taking it one step at a time,
I seek the desires of my heart.
And my dreams are not far away
To be fulfilled.

Recovering from it all,
I pick up the scattered pieces
Along the way.
Drifting away-far too long,
I now re-group, to get some balance.
And I'm ready to begin again.
Out Here-
Gathering Stones

His Everlasting Love

It is our Faith through every moment of the day-
that we hold on to. For His Everlasting Love –
will always be there through the sunshine and through the rain.

A White Rose Of Hope

As we look across the way-
With the dark clouds upon us-
I Pray for *Hope.*

Hope for brighter days ahead.
Hope as we face storms coming
In every direction-
We endure.

We can press forward each day-
To never give up-
And to always give the best of ourselves.

And with the belief that soon,
And the dark clouds will be no more -
We hold on to His Grace –
As we look across the way-
We see –
A White Rose of Hope.

Each Day I Go Forward

I've decided not to worry about things
I cannot change.
Only to spend the time on things I can.

I've decided not to concern myself
Who loves me?
Only to let the love to always shine inside of me.

I've decided not to put much importance
On trivial things-
Only to understand what's most important
At the moment.

I've decided not to let negative thinking come
Inside of me.
Only to allow positive thinking in my heart.

I've decided not to let life's challenges
Doubt my *faith*.
Only to find strength through it all-
Always keeping the *faith*.

And most importantly-
I've decided no matter what
I may be going through-
I will always put my trust in Him –
Each Day I Go Forward

Always There

You're always there through every trial,
Every triumph,
Your Peace I find.
I lift my head up high,
Knowing my help comes from-
You.

I Praise You,
Every minute,
Every hour,
Every day.
For You're always there,
Guiding me through it all.
Reassuring me so much.

You're my salvation,
My joy in the morning
To hold me as the evening comes,
And on to the next new day.

There's so much I can say about You.
Your Goodness,
Your Grace.
And I Thank You
To Know-
You're-
Always There.

As A Flower Blooms – Hope Lives

There's always *Hope* to hold on to.
And each time the rain comes-
The sun will shine even more brighter.

Sometimes life may throw us a curve.
All of a sudden it may seem difficult
To grasp.
But with hope and always faith-
We can know *joy* in every precious moment.

For as we have each morning-
As we awake each day –
Each time the sun rises –
Each time a flower blooms-
There's always *Hope* to hold on to.
For-
As A Flower Blooms – Hope Lives.

I Abide In You

You are the *joy* in the morning.
You are the *strength* I need each day.
You are the *wind* that holds me through every storm.

You are the *light* through the darkness.
You are the *sunshine* through the rain.
You are the *anchor* when the waters overflow.
And when *danger* is near,
Your arms surround me to know
You will never leave me.

For it's my *faith* that keeps me going.
It's my *trust* in You-
The reassurance,
The peace within my soul
That wherever I am-
Dear Lord!
I believe things that seem impossible -
Are possible always-
With You!

In Due Season

When I think about all the blessings
He brings.
When I think about His Grace-
His Love-
I can only stay where He wants me to be.
I cannot doubt Him,
No matter what,
No matter the challenges.
And when the storms come,
And it seems as though they will not pass,
I look up to Him to know
He's my help,
He's my friend.
And whatever my desires,
I know He will grant.
Yes,
Always-
In Due Season

The Lord Watches Over Me

I do not fear the darkness at night.
For the sparrow stays within my sight.
Oh! How The Lord Watches Over Me.

I do not fear the arrows that come at me
During the day.
For the Lord is all around,
He is with me in every way.
The Lord Watches Over Me.

I do not dwell too long in despair.
For I know I am in the Lord's care.
The Lord He Watches Over Me.

I trust in the Lord, I hold on to His
Unchanging hand.
For when I am weak, He helps me stand.
The Lord Watches Over Me.

I will stay in the house of the Lord,
He will never leave me.
For I know with Faith,
He is with me through eternity.
Oh! How The Lord Watches Over Me.

God Answers Prayers

The Lord will make a way through no way.
For when the storms come – Pray!

Hold on to Hope, when all seems gone.
For when you are weak,
He will keep you strong.

Always have *Faith* in the Lord.
He takes care of all things.
Trust in Him.
His Love and Mercy are forever.

He will make a way through no way.
For as you leave things with Him,
He will see you through any storm.
For-
He Answers Prayers

Blessings

The sun shining all the time
Life through devastation
Seeing a newborn child
Prayers answered over and over again
Giving life back
Finding peace
Children laughing and playing
A smile
Being in Love
Seizing the moments
The Love of a Mother
A Father's joy
A child's gift
Family Gatherings
Friendship
Seeing an old friend
Unexpected presents
A bouquet of flowers
Pink Roses
Snow on Christmas Day
Spring in Washington DC
A rainbow after the rain
Summer Breezes
A Thank you for no reason

Encouragement
Fulfillment
Inspirational messages
A pat on the back
A Hug
Congratulations!
A listening ear
A helping hand
An understanding heart
Love-
Blessings!

His Everlasting Love

There's always a *Blessing* He brings,
In every moment of each day.
For no matter, what life brings
From day to day,
And whether it seems hopeless
Beyond despair,
Know that His Love will never fail us,
And that we can find strength for the day.

As we hold on to *Hope*-
As we believe tomorrow will be better –
May we trust in *Faith*-
That His Mercy-
His Everlasting Love will be there-
Always –
For every moment of each day.

As I Plant The Seeds
Of My Garden

I am finding great achievements comes-
with courage and the belief in you.
And as I plant the seeds of my garden –
I live my dreams possible to become true.

The Love Inside Of You

Take the disappointments
And make them your blessings.
Always stay positive no matter
What each day brings.

For it's all up to you.
You always have a choice
To live a full or half full life.

Rise above what you cannot change.
And focus on what you can.
For yesterday is past,
And today is a new day.

There's always a blessing through
Every experience.
And with each experience –
There's always something you can learn.

Live each day as if it's your last.
Press forward with faith.
And most importantly –
Always Keep-
The Love Inside of You.

A Journey Of A Thousand Steps

You must never give up when it seems so far.
You must never doubt when it all seems it's going nowhere.
You must never say you can't-always say you can.
It doesn't matter how long the journey.
What matters that you give it your all,
All the way to the end.
A true winner never gives up,
Never doubts when things go wrong.
Always gearing with positive energy,
No matter how the road turns.
For one single step leads to a thousand steps,
Making dreams come true.

The Beauty Of You

As you come to love who you are-
All you can give-
The beauty of you will shine even more.

Only you can define the gift
That is yours alone.
And when you begin to see the inner you-
Having the faith in all you can be.
You can rise above any challenge imaginable.

As you come to love who you are-
As you embrace your own uniqueness-
You will always give the best of who you are.
And the beauty of you will always-
Shine Through!

I Cannot Stay Where I Am

This change I find in me,
Empowers me to never give up.
To endure,
With Faith.
And whatever obstacles along the way,
I can overcome.
Today, I own this for self,
And go forward with a new vision
To know all things, I dream for,
Hope for,
I can achieve.
I cannot stay where I am.
And I Thank You Lord for This.

Inspiration

To believe all is possible,
That seems impossible,
To always encourage,
To enlighten the spirit,
To spread a little love wherever you go.
And just maybe as you pass it on,
The world will be more beautiful.
And before you know what a difference
You've made.
A more beautiful world you can ever
Have dreamed.
If you could only imagine
Such an inspiration that would be?

The Leap Of Faith

Take the leap of *faith* and believe
Each step you take empowers you
To go the distance.
Find strength through each challenge
You so endure.
And when disappointments come,
Receive them as blessings
To keep going even more.
Never give up,
No matter what comes your way,
No matter how difficult the climb.
Just know as you keep going,
His Mercy,
His Love,
Will never fail you.
Take the Leap of Faith
And –*Believe.*

To Fly Like An Eagle

To fly like an eagle
Is to follow one's dreams
For however long it takes you.
Always daring about new adventures beyond
Your imagination.

To fly like an eagle
Is never giving up when the distance seems so far.
Moving beyond the barriers, the obstacles.
Stead fast with self-determination.

To fly like an eagle
Is to believe you can do all you dream to be.
Keeping your spirits high with positive energy,
Always giving your best!

To fly like an eagle
Is believing each step you take,
Brings you closer that all is possible,
Beyond and Beyond!
Just Fly Like an Eagle!

Words Of Encouragement

I awake this day encouraged.
To know I can do all things possible with You.
For I cannot go back to where I was.
Nor can I stay where I am.
But as I move forward-
I hold on to the promise.

Your blessings never cease.
And Your Enduring Promise is the reassurance -
There's nothing You can't do.

I can rise above any storm imaginable.
I can overcome any obstacle.
My faith is renewed.
And more than ever before I trust in-You!
I Awake Each Day-
Encouraged!

True Beauty

The *true beauty* is always inside of you.
That inner spirit that we all have.
To like who you are.
To find your own gift.
And discover your own uniqueness.

Know that you are already beautiful
With what He has given only to you.
For we all have *a purpose-*
A *passion* to fulfill in this life.

And we all have a choice to live our dreams-
To give the best of ourselves-
Our gift to the world.

For as you start to see the *true beauty*
That is inside of you.
You'll be able to let others see it too.
For the *True Beauty* is always –
Yes Always! –
Inside of – you.

There's A Beautiful Voice Inside Of Me

There's a beautiful voice inside of me-
Instilling my faith in You.
And I thank you for every challenge –
Every *joy* in my life.

For with every challenge-
There's *A Blessing* every time.
And for every joy there's the reassurance –
You're always there with no doubt.

There's a beautiful voice inside of me,
That when things are not going well-
You give me the strength to see it through.
And more than ever *I Praise You* even more.

There's a beautiful voice inside of me,
That encourages me to go even further
Than I can ever have dreamed imaginable.
For all things are possible with You.

There's a beautiful voice inside of me-
Instilling my faith in You.
And Dear Lord!-
I thank You for every challenge –
Every joy in my life.
There's A Beautiful Voice Inside of Me!

A Rainbow Of Hope

There will be storms, but they do not last forever.
Hold on to A Rainbow of Hope – and always Pray!
      For through every storm imaginable – there's always-
      A Blessing He brings.

Where's There's Hope-There's Love

There are days when the sun does not shine.
And sometimes there will be clouds
And the rain will follow.
But where there's Hope-there's Love.

For even at those most difficult times,
And the rain seems as though it will never end.
Believe there's always Hope-
And the Love He has for you.

Life's most difficult challenge is-
A test of faith.
And as you endure-
He will see you through.
You will survive!

For even on those most cloudy of days-
Believe that the sun will shine tomorrow.

There's Always A Season

There's always a season for all things.
There'll be challenges – as well as triumphs.
And sometimes the disappointments come-
To test your *Faith*.

Always stay encouraged no matter
What you're going through.
Welcome the blessings as they come.
And when it seems as though there's
Not much love around-
Let the *Love* shine in you even more.

Things don't always stay the same
As the day before.
Know He will give you the desires of your heart.
Be hopeful each and every day.
For-
There's Always A Season For All Things.

The Storms

He didn't promise they'll always be days of sunshine.
For rainy days do come.
And sometimes they may seem to last forever.

Believe He will always be there
To get you through any storm.
Yes! – any storm imaginable.

Sometimes storms may be a test of one's faith.
For as you trust in Him-
To know with no doubt
All will be alright-no matter how heavy the storm.

He will carry you when you cannot carry yourself.
He will bring you through.
Even if it seems hopeless.
Know that He is *hope* to hold on to.

He didn't promise they'll always be days of sunshine.
But He did promise
He will always be there through it all.
For He will bring a *Blessing* through –
The Storms.

Hold On To The Sunshine After The Rain

We can see the sunshine after the rain.
And no matter how difficult
The storm,
It will be alright.

We can find strength for each day-
As we hold on to *His Promise*-
For He'll carry us through
With *His Mercy-His Love* so dear.

We can see the light through the darkness.
And believe with the astounding *faith*-
That He'll always be there-*Always*.

We can rise above any storm imaginable-
For with Him all things are possible.
Yes! All things are possible with- *Hope.*
And we can see the sunshine-
After The Rain

God's Peace

When the world seems too much to bear -
Too much to grasp -
I seek Your Peace within.
I find Your Strength to sustain me at all times.
And I pray more than ever before.
For it's Your Peace that flows like
The water along any brook or stream.
It's Your Peace that makes the new fallen snow
So beautiful on a brisk winter's morning.
It's Your Peace when the birds sing so lovely
On a warm summer's day.
It's Your Peace when the leaves fall
So gently in October.
It's Your Peace so beautiful.
When the world seems too much to bear -
Too much to grasp-
I look up to know You're always there.
With You-
Such Peace-
I Find.

Hope

Giving up is surrender to no place.
When all seems lost, holding on
Brings you one step closer to the promise.
And as you believe each day is a new day,
Your trials can be your triumph.
Just believe that it all gets better,
No matter your circumstance,
No matter what you go through.
Believe what is now can change tomorrow.
Believe with Faith.
And always hold on to-
Hope.

So Beautiful The River Each Time It Flows

The river is so beautiful each time it flows.
And on this day, I seek You more.
There's a peace that I so find-
As the waters of the river flows so calm-so serene.

All is well.
And when the challenges come,
I seek You more than ever in this quiet place
Where the river flows.
I hold on to hope that tomorrow will be better.
For today is a test of my faith.

Things do not stay the same.
Each day is new.
And there's always a blessing You bring
Each day in one's life.

On this day, I seek You more.
I Hold On.
I Hold on to-You!

Oh! How beautiful the river-
Each Time It Flows.

I Wish To Live Life

I want to receive the Lord's Blessings every day.
I want to be at my best,
Even if I'm at my worst in every way.

I want to hold on to only good feelings in my heart.
I want to move on from disappointments,
As I make a new start.

I want to be receptive of change and not lose me.
I want to always in every situation,
Open my eyes and see.

I want to look back at the past to reflect,
And not feel sorrow.
I want to hold on to hope,
As I look forward to tomorrow.

I want to always to *"keep the faith"*
For dreams to come true.
I want to not remain sad, lonely, and blue.

I want to always let positive thinking
In my life play a vital part.
And-
I want to always have *Love* in my heart.
For-
I Wish To Live Life!

A Rainbow Of Hope

Storms do come your way.
Some seems as though they last forever.
But hold on to Hope through the storms-
As they come through.

Hold on to His Everlasting Mercy – His Love.
And always Pray!
Know that each day you have - is a blessing -
A rainbow of Hope - in giving you strength -
And the resolve through it all.

Always stay in Faith and believe-
That what seems hopeless-
He is the Hope for you to never doubt
His Amazing Love.

Storms do not last forever.
And His Love will see you through every storm.
Hold on to the Blessing-
A Rainbow of Hope –
He brings each day you breathe – *Life!*

Over The Horizon

Each morning as the sun rises-each night as the sun sets-
And as we look Over the Horizon-may we come to know − Love.

Each Day I Hope – I Pray!

Each day I Hope-I Pray-
That those in higher places-
Always answers to their hearts.

Each day I Hope-I Pray-
That no matter those positions-
Those statues each one holds-
To do the right thing is the best thing for us all.

Each day I Hope-I Pray-
That no matter what the agenda for the day-
It serves no purpose when it hurts so many.

Each day I Hope-I Pray-
That as we come with understanding-
As we stand together no matter our differences-
We will survive anything.

Each day I Hope-I Pray-
That the love of Humanity-
Always outweighs anything else.

Each day I Hope-I Pray-
That we will crush hate to the ground-
For Love will save us.

Each day I Hope-I Pray!-
As the sun rises-and as the sun sets-
We will come to see most of all-*Love!*-
Is the only thing that matters.

For Every Moment Of Each Day – I Pray!

For every moment of each day-
I say a prayer for the world.
And as I look over the horizon,
I can see a more beautiful world.

Yes a more beautiful world.
Even at the most difficult times,
Even when there seems not much
Hope to hold on to-
I hold on to hope
For brighter days ahead.

For without faith and hope
To hold on to-
I believe we will come to an
Understanding that *Love* itself
Is far greater than anything.

For every moment of each day-
I say a prayer for the world.
And as I look over the horizon -
I can see a more beautiful world.
For every moment of each day-
I Pray!

Turns

Plans can be changed.
Nothing is certain, or final.
One does not know
What's beyond the horizon?
For what is today,
May not be your tomorrow.

Doors do open,
And doors close.
And those doors that close-
May open again.

Disappointments will come,
And sometimes all at once.
And blessings will also come
When you least expect to make
It all worthwhile.

Things can remain the same,
And things can change in one minute.
And when things are similar,
The outcome may not be the same.

Each Day is new,
And one can always *hope*.
For Life has its-
Turns

Where The Grass Is Green

There has to be a place-Where the Grass Is Green,
Where Love is-always love.

There has to be a place-Where the Grass is Green,
Where I can be me,
And not concern myself if it's ok.

There has to be a place-Where the Grass is Green,
Where patience lies,
And positive energy spreads in every direction.

There has to be a place-Where the Grass is Green,
Where there's no fear to live each day,
And to trust is common practice.

There has to be a place-Where the Grass is Green,
Where the quality of life is abundant,
And working hard has more value.

There has to be a place – Where the Grass is Green,
Where war is just a distant memory of yesterday.
And peace is something we don't have to dream about.

There has to be a place-Where the Grass is Green,
Where Love keeps growing-
Crushing hate to the ground.

There has to be a place-Where the Grass is Green,
Where love is-always *Love.*
There has to be a place-
Where The Grass Is Green.

All Of A Sudden

Children will no longer be killing children.
All of A Sudden
Families will spend more time together, not apart.
All of A Sudden

People will start to talk and not argue.
All of A Sudden

Police will serve and protect all their citizens,
No matter race or disability.
All of A Sudden

There will be no more hunger in the land.
All of A Sudden

There will be a cure for cancer and the sick
Will have hope.
All of A Sudden

All of us will have a better quality of life.
All of A Sudden

There will be no more hate, only love.
For before you know it-*God's Love*
Will conquer all.
All of A Sudden

Always Love

Sometimes you may not see *Love* present.
And sometimes love seems as though
It doesn't stay around too long.
But when you find there's no Love around-
Hold on to it more than ever.
It's the only thing that-Last.

The world cannot live without Love-
And what's so amazing-
It never lets you down.
The more you invite love -
The more you share love-
Wonderful things happen!

Never give up on *Love.*
Hold on to it more than ever-
For it's the only thing that *-Last!*

New Life

As I move towards a new way of thinking – positive-
Leaving all old habits of negativity behind me.
I can discover new oceans with a sense of direction.
Going forward I can plainly see – the sunset-the blue skies.

Oh, how beautiful it is to see God's creation.
For Life is so precious to waste even a minute
Of its treasures to go by.

As I stop and take time to smell the roses –
I have a smile on my face –
With Love in my heart for others –
For this I must try.
In knowing I can always begin again.
In an effort towards being the best I can be-
To seek salvation –
To live a better way.

And as I find complete serenity
Within my heart –
For then I can say –
This is a wonderful –
New Life.

Home

Balancing it all together,
What makes sense is the
Purpose of why I'm here.
Where I am meant to be-
At peace always,
In my soul always.
And yes,
Love I find everywhere.
While other things come and go,
Love never dies!
I see the morning sun,
I start a new day.
And it's all because of You.
You have given me new life.
Much greater than I can ever imagine.
It never left me.
Though at times I've moved away from it.
And this is where I will stay.
So glad I found my way back-*here.*
Dear Lord!
So glad I'm-
Home.

Over The Horizon

Even if the rain seems to last forever-
The sun will always shine through.
Always there's a test in your faith.
And time shows that so well.

There are no barriers you cannot overcome.
And as each morning the sun rises-
Each night the sun sets-
Stay Encouraged!

Hold on to your faith.
Find strength through the day.
Believe all things work out.
Press forward with Hope.

For the rain may seem to last forever-
But as you look-
Over the Horizon-
The sun always shines through.

Closing Poem

Beyond The Sunset

As I look beyond the beautiful skies-
Before the night begins to fall-
I hold on to *hope* for brighter tomorrows.

Where hope lies-
I believe we can hold on to love.
For *hope* invites us to know-*Love!*

Love! is our true salvation.
Love will never fail us-
Only encourages us to see
Its beauty-
To give the best of ourselves-
To always answer to our hearts.

Love will always be there
For each of us to embrace.
And as we come to love
One another –
To believe in its promise-
Love! we can come to know-
Beyond The Sunset.

Printed in the United States
By Bookmasters